# THE ADVANCED SHOTOKAN KARATE HANDBOOK

# GICHIN FUNAKOSHI

*Father of modern-day Karate*

**1868-1957**

Pictured above is Gichin Funakoshi, the father of modern-day Karate. In addition to Karate, he was deeply involved in calligraphy and the writing of poetry. He would sign his work by using his pen name, Shoto. It is from that pen name that the creation of the word "Shotokan" arose. The name is made up using the word Shoto, meaning waving pines (his verse was often inspired by the gently waving pines on the hills near his home), and the word Kan, meaning house or school. His first school of Karate, based at his home, therefore became known as Shoto's Kan, which was eventually shortened to Shotokan.

In 1955, the Japan Karate Association was established with Funakoshi as Chief Instructor.

The handful of students and instructors who trained under him then passed their experience and knowledge on to the continuing stream of hungry, prospective Karate-Kas. Funakoshi, remembered as the master of Karate, died in 1957 at the age of 88.

# THE ADVANCED SHOTOKAN KARATE HANDBOOK

By
**GURSHARAN SAHOTA**
**6th Dan**

**CHIEF INSTRUCTOR**
**TRADITIONAL INTERNATIONAL SHOTOKAN KARATE ASSOCIATION**

Published By
**GURSHARAN SAHOTA**
www.Tiska.com

First Published May 1997
Second reprint 2005


By the Same Author
The Shotokan Karate Handbook - Beginner to Black Belt

## ACKNOWLEDGEMENTS

The author wishes to thank the following:
The association Black Belts namely; Pedro Barker, Kevin Coles, Carole Barker, Patricia Ferguson (Bahamas), Martin Palfrey, Colin Thorp, Paul Leon, Kevin Anderson, Paul Debock, Samantha Lavender,  Derek Brogie, Martin Toyer, Alison Csom, Christopher Moody, Emma Rogers, Manpreet Sehmbi, Charlene Lowde, Katie Woodland, and Patricia Blaney. Roy Hazelwood, Chief Instructor of

Traditional Shotokan Karate Association (GB), Lawrence Elcock, Chief Instructor of C.M.K. for their enthusiasm and support, as always.

Paul Hooley, for his technical advice in producing this book. Alan Cooke of A C Photography, for his patience during the lengthy photo sessions and last but not least Jacqui Malam for all her invaluable help.

*ISBN 0 9524638 1 4*

*Published by Gursharan Sahota, email: tiska.karate@btinternat.com*
*www.tiska.com*

**U.K. Distributor:**
*Gazelle Book Services Limited, Falcon House, Queen Square, Lancaster LA1 1RN, England.*
*Telephone No: 01524-68765  Fax No: 01524-63232*

**U.S.A. Distributor:**
*National Book Network, 230 Commercial Street, Boston, MA 02109*
*Telephone No: (617) 557-4176 Fax No: (617) 557-4176*

**Martial Arts Trade Distributors:**
*Giko,35 Litchfield Road, Birmingham B65 RW*
*Telephone No: 0121-327-8880 Fax No: 0121-327-8881*

*Produced by Paul Hooley and Associates, Bedford, England*
*Printed in China*

I dedicate this book to my brothers and sisters
AVTAR, BHUPINDER, ABNASH, and DASHVINDER

# PREFACE

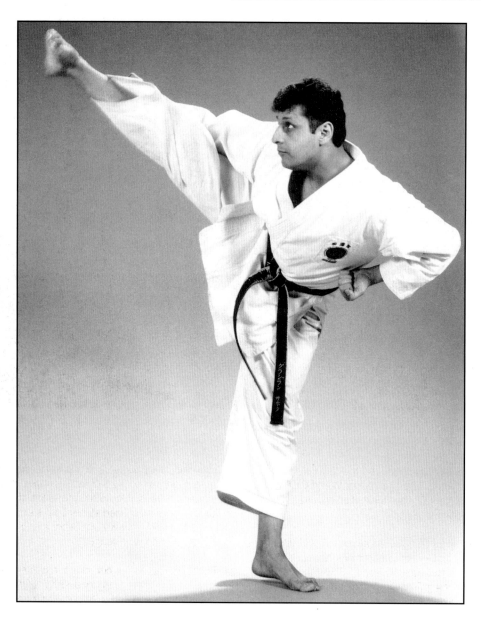

**GURSHARAN SAHOTA –5th DAN**

Following the success of my first book, *The Shotokan Karate Handbook – Beginner to Black Belt*, I felt there was a need for a manual to assist the more experienced student.

Therefore, I have concentrated on more advanced techniques such as Kihon Ippon Kumite, Jiyu Ippon Kumite sets 6 & 7, and all the remaining Katas in Shotokan Karate.

As I stated in my first book, it is important that Karate Ka are

aware that time, effort and practice are still the main factors in working towards perfecting not only one's skills but also one's inner mind and attitude towards an Art.

This book is meant as a guide to Karate Ka – It cannot take the place of your Sensei (teacher).

*GURSHARAN SAHOTA*
*April 1997*

# FOREWORD

As a sports writer who has covered the Olympic Games, boxing world title fights and the soccer World Cup, I am acutely aware of the skill and dedication required to succeed at the highest levels of sport.

So, too, is Gursharan Sahota, an athlete as skilfull and dedicated as any I have come across in 30 years as a newspaperman. Since he is blessed with such qualities in abundance, it was perfectly natural that he should be one of the leading Karate-Ka in Britain during the past 24 years.

I have known Gursharan for 12 of those years, and it was clear from the start that the was destined for great things. It was certainly no surprise when TISKA, the association he formed in 1993, quickly blossomed into a major organisation with branches internationally and throughout the United Kingdom.

The man is a natural leader and teacher whose instruction can only be of assistance to Karate-Ka of all grades. there is little doubt, therefore, that this manual for the more advanced student will be an invaluable aid for all those Karate-Ka who want to improve their technique and knowledge.

The following pages containing extemely detailed explicit step by step easy to follow photographs in Kumite, Kata and Bunkai, to assist a Karate-Ka's personal achievement in the study of this fascinating Art of Shotokan Karate.

COLIN MALAM
*Sunday Telegraph*

# THE HISTORY OF KARATE

The two Chinese characters **KARA** and **TE** make up the ideographs in Japan for the word Karate, and thus denote that it is of Chinese origin. It appears that this evidence points towards the fact that Karate was practised in China first before it was ever practised in Japan or the Ryukyu Islands.

It is known that, in the Sixth Century, an Indian Buddhist Monk, Bodhidharma, journeyed from Asia to China. His role was to establish the Zen School of Buddhism.

Bodhidharma travelled to the Shaolin Temple, where his teaching began. Many of the monks were very weak and found such physical exercise too exhausting.

Bodhidharma devised a training method that would assist the monks both physically and mentally so that they could continue their Zen practice.

The word Karate means "empty hand" – Kara meaning empty and Te meaning hand. It is an art which teaches its students self defence by using their arms and legs as controlled weapons.

The master behind Karate was Gichin Funakoshi. He was born in Shuri, Okinawa Prefecture in 1868. It was whilst he was lecturing at the Okinawa Teachers' College that he was given the opportunity, in 1922, to lecture and demonstrate his art of Karate. The event was sponsored by the Ministry of Education. After such a demonstration, Funakoshi received a multitude of requests for him to teach in Tokyo.

In 1936 Funakoshi formed "Shotokan", a true landmark in Karate's history.

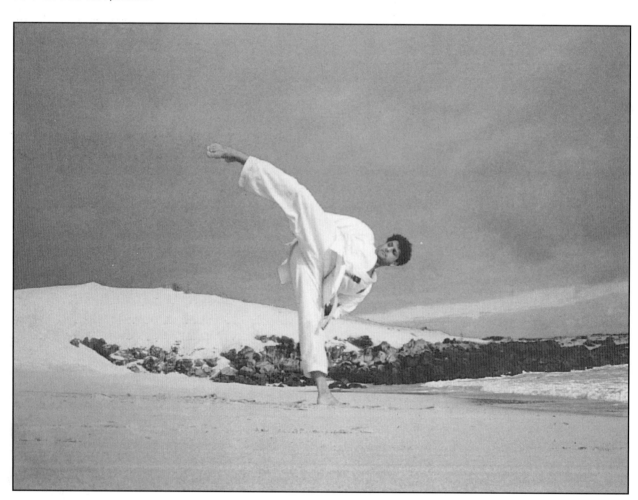

*Gursharan Sahota demonstrating Ushiro Mawashi Geri*

# CONTENTS

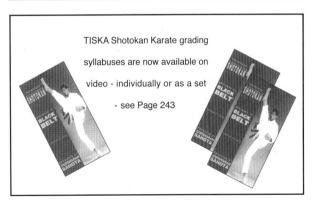

TISKA Shotokan Karate grading syllabuses are now available on video - individually or as a set - see Page 243

## THE KUMITE TEAM

**Gursharan Sahota (Team Captain), Roy Hazelwood, Donovan Slue,
Robin Reid, & Lawrence Elcock**

# KUMITE
## *Sparring*

Kumite (sparring) is divided into various categories of pre-arranged sparring. Namely: Gohon Kumite – five-attack sparring Sanbon Kumite – three-attack sparring, Kihon Ippon Kumite – basic one-attack sparring, Kaeshi Ippon Kumite – basic one-attack sparring (with returning step counter-attack), Jiyu Ippon Kumite – semi free one-attack sparring, Okuri Jiyu Ippon Kumite (as Jiyu Ippon, but with a second free attack) and finally Jiyu Kumite – freestyle, which enables the Karate-Ka to use freely any of the aforementioned techniques against their opponent without warning. At all times, you should remember to take into consideration the essence of Karate-Do, i.e. "Karate ni sentanashi", there is no first attack in Karate.

# SANBON KUMITE: *3 Attack Sparring*

SANBON Kumite is a 3-attack sparring combination. The procedure is almost identical to Gohon Kumite, with the exception that the attack levels may be Jodan, Chudan or Mae Geri, or any combination of the three (as illustrated in this section). The defensive sequence is Age Uke, Soto Ude Uke and Gedan Barai with Gyaku Zuki as the counter-attack.

1. YOI

2. The person attacking steps back into Gedan Barai

3. Oi Zuki Jodan | Hidari Age Uke

4. Oi Zuki Chudan | Migi Soto Ude Uke

5. Mae Geri Chudan | Hidari Gedan Barai

6. Right Gyaku Zuki counter attack with **KIAI**

7. Yame

Both pulling up into YOI

# SANBON KUMITE: Set 2

1. Attacker steps back into Gedan Barai.

2. Jodan Oi Zuki | Hidari Age Uke

3. Chudan Oi Zuki | Uchi Ude Uke

4. Chudan Mae Geri | Gyaku Gedan Barai

5. Left Jodan | Kizami Zuki

6. Chudan Gyaku Zuki counter attack **KIAI**

1. Attacker steps back in Gedan Barai

2. Jodan Oi Zuki | Haiwan Uke – Kokutsu Dachi

3. Chudan Oi Zuki | Morote Uke – Kokutsu Dachi

4. Chudan Mae Geri | Sukui Uke– Kokutsu Dachi

5. Chudan Gyaku Zuki counter attack **KIAI**

# SANBON KUMITE: Set 4

1. Attacker steps back into Gedan Barai

2. Jodan Oi Zuki | Jodan Haishu Uke

3. Intermediate movement

4. Chudan Oi Zuki | Uchi Ude Uke

5. Chudan Mae Geri | Kaki Uke

6. Intermediate movement. Spinning round.

7. Jodan Empi Uchi **KIAI**

1. Attacker steps back into Jiyu Dachi

2. Chudan Oi Zuki | Te Negashi Uke

3. Intermediate movement

4. Jodan Oi Zuki | Jiyu Dachi

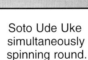

5. Chudan Oi Zuki | Soto Ude Uke simultaneously spinning round.

6. Intermediate movement

7. Chudan Oi Zuki | Jiyu Dachi

8. Chudan Mae Geri | Kake Uke

9. Pulling front foot back as per arrow

10. Uraken Jodan

11. Chudan Gyaku
    Zuki **KIAI**

12. Jiyu Dachi
    Hikite Gamae

# KIHON IPPON KUMITE : *Basic 1 Attack Sparring*

Kihon Ippon Kumite, (basic one-attack sparring), allows both opponents to attack in turn. Although pre-arranged techniques are used to defend and counter-attack, it is not always necessary to defend in a straight line. Thus, side-stepping and moving at 45-degree angles can be very effective in this exercise.

Kihon Ippon Kumite begins with the attacker in Gedan Barai and the defender in the Yoi position. The defender, having completed his or her counter-attack with Kiai,

returns to the Yoi position. Under no circumstances must he or she pull into the free-style (Jiyu Dachi stance).

It is essential that the attack is strong at all times. He or she should exercise control when aiming for the face, but some contact ought to be made if possible when attacking the mid-section. On no account should the defender follow through and make contact. After blocking, he or she should focus his or her counter-attack just short of the target.

# KIHON IPPON KUMITE: SET 6

**JODAN**

1. YOI | Gedan Barai

2. Haishu Uke | Jodan Oi Zuki

3. Swing Arm over and implement armlock. | Jodan Oi Zuki

4. Gyaku Zuki Chudan

5. Grab hold of head

6. Pull down Hiza Geri **KIAI**

---

*The Advanced Shotokan Karate Handbook*

**CHUDAN**

1. YOI | Step back
Gedan Barai

2. Gedan Barai
feet ending up
together | Chudan Oi Zuki

3. Chudan Kekomi

4.  Intermediate movement

5.  Jodan Shuto Uke

6.  Chudan Gyaku Zuki **KIAI**

**MAE GERI**

| 1. YOI | Attacker steps back into Zenkutsu Dachi | 2. Gedan Barai | Mae Geri Chudan | 3. Pull foot back for kicking distance. |

4. Mae Geri Chudan

5. Oi Zuki Jodan **KIAI**

**KEKOMI**

1. Attacker steps back into Zenkutsu Dachi | YOI

2. Intermediate movement

3. Yoko Geri Kekomi | Sliding through Gedan Barai

4. Spinning round

5. Jodan Empi Uchi **KIAI**

**MAWASHI GERI**

1. YOI | Attacker steps back into Zenkutsu Dachi

2. Gyaku Uchi Uke | Mawashi Geri

3. Kizami Zuki Jodan

4. Gyaku Zuki Chudan
   **KIAI**

**JODAN**

1. YOI      Attacker steps
back into
Gedan Barai

2. Te Negashi    Oi Zuki Jodan
Uke

3. Intermediate movement

4. Uraken Jodan

5. Intermediate movement

6. Gedan Tetsui Uchi **KIAI**

**CHUDAN**

1. YOI | Attacker steps back into Gedan Barai

2. Intermediate movement Stepping Forward

3. Tetsui Uchi Jodan Same motion as Kosa Uke

4. Grab head

5. Pull down Hiza Geri
   **KIAI**

**MAE GERI**

1. Attacker steps | Yoi
   back into
   Zenkutsu
   Dachi

2. Mae Geri | Gyaku Gedan
   Chudan | Barai

3. Jodan Mawashi Empi

4. Gyaku Ura Zuki
   **KIAI**

**KEKOMI**

1. YOI | Attacker steps back into Zenkutsu Dachi

2. Kake Uke | Yoko Geri Kekomi

3. Pulling right foot back

4. Intermediate movement

5. Left Ushiro Geri
   **KIAI**

**MAWASHI GERI**

1. YOI | Attacker steps back into Zenkutsu Dachi

2. Gyaku Haishu Uke | Mawashi Geri

3. Chudan Maegeri

4. Intermediate movement

5. Uraken Jodan

6. Gyaku Zuki Chudan
   **KIAI**

# JIYU IPPON KUMITE: *Semi Free 1 Attack Sparring*

Jiyu Ippon Kumite is halfway between Kihon Ippon Kumite and Jiyu Kumite. Up to now, the overriding theme of all the different forms of Kumite training has been one of formality.

Jiyu Ippon Kumite, is performed in 'Jiyu Dachi', or free-fighting stance, the attack is pre-arranged. The defence and counter-attack are of the defender's own choosing, after which he or she returns to Jiyu Dachi, Hikite Gamae.
Jiyu Ippon Kumite requires any defender to think for themselves, rather than follow an instruction. Timing and distancing are important for both attacker and defender. Indeed, timing is vital for the attacker.

Tai Sabaki, or body shifting, is particularly effective in this context. It allows the defender to move in virtually any direction to evade attack before counter-attacking.

In Jiyu Ippon Kumite, it is possible to increase the power of your counter-attack by using an opponent's power and speed against them. You can increase your chances of success too by watching your opponent's breathing then attacking while he or she is inhaling.

**JODAN**

1. Jiyu Dachi

2. Oi Zuki Jodan | Dropping down, left hand Shuto Uke, right hand Gyaku Zuki

3. Intermediate movement. Sliding forward, right hand in position for Sukui Uke

4. Ashi Barai

5. Intermediate movement

6. Shuto Uchi
   **KIAI**

7. Jiyu Dachi

---

**CHUDAN**

1. Jiyu Dachi

2. Oi Zuki Chudan | Shuffle stance left Te Osai Uke

3. Uraken Jodan while landing

4. Intermediate movement

5. Grabbing hold

6. Intermediate movement

7. Ashi Barai

8. Intermediate movement

9. Gyaku Zuki
   **KIAI**

**CHUDAN**

10.  Hikite Gamae

**MAE GERI**

1. Jiyu Dachi

2. Gyaku Gedan
   Barai
   Te Uke for
   safety

   Mae Geri
   Chudan

3. Intermediate ready to sweep

4. Ashi Barai

5. Intermediate movement

6. Gyaku Zuki
   **KIAI**

7. Hikite Gamae

**KEKOMI**

1. Jiyu Dachi

2. Intermediate movement

3. Yoko Geri Kekomi | Gedan Barai

4. Sukui Uke

5. Ashi Barai

6. Awase Uki
   **KIAI**

7. Hikite Gamae

## MAWASHI GERI

1. Jiyu Dachi

2. Jump & change stance

3. Sinking down | Leg in position for Mawashi Geri

4. Ready for Ashi Barai | Mawashi Geri

5. Ashi Barai

6. Intermediate movement

7. Kakato Geri
   **KIAI**

**USHIRO GERI**

1. Jiyu Dachi

2. Ushiro Geri  |  Kake Uke

3. Pull left foot back

4. Ushiro Mawashi Geri

5. Ready for Ashi Barai

6. Ashi Barai

7. Gyaku Zuki
   **KIAI**

# JIYU IPPON KUMITE: SET 7

**JODAN**

1. Jiyu Dachi

2. Jump on spot changing stance, left Negashi Uke | Attacking Oi Zuki Jodan

3. Left hand Negashi Uke right Ura Zuki

4. Grabbing hold under arm

5. Stepping round with left foot

6. Using hip and throwing

7. Intermediate movement ready for Kakato Geri

8. Kakato Geri
**KIAI**

**CHUDAN**

1. Jiyu Dachi

2. Oi Zuki          | Gedan
   Chudan           | Barai

3. Kizami Chudan Mawashigeri

4. Intermediate movement

5. Uraken Uchi Jodan

6. Intermediate movement ready for Ashi Barai

7. Ashi Barai

8. Gyaku Zuki

9. Hikite Gamae

**MAE GERI**

1. Jiyu Dachi

2. Ready for Gedan Barai pulling left foot back | Intermediate movement

3. Gedan Barai preparing for Mawashi Geri | Mae Geri

4. Chudan Mawashi Geri

5. Ashi Barai while landing

6. Gyaku Zuki Chudan

7. Hikite Gamae

**KEKOMI**

1. Jiyu Dachi

2. Kake Uke | Yoko Geri Kekomi

3. Intermediate movement spinning round

4. Preparing for Ashi Barai

5. Ashi Barai

6. Gyaku Zuki
   **KIAI**

7. Hikite Gamae

**MAWASHI GERI**

1. Jiyu Dachi

2.  | Intermediate movement

3. Lean back Gyaku Sukui Uke | Mawashi Geri

4. Kizami Zuki Jodan

5. Preparing for Ashi Barai

6. Ashi Barai

7. Intermediate movement Preparing for Kakato Geri

8. Kakato Geri
   **KIAI**

**USHIRO GERI**

1. Jiyu Dachi

2. Kake Uke   |   Ushiro Geri

3. Spinning round

4. Preparing for Ushiro Geri

5. Ushiro Geri
   **KIAI**

*It will take your entire life to learn
karate: there is no limit*

# KATA
## *Formal Exercise*

Kata, which means formal exercise, consists of a set number of pre-determined moves which are designed to be performed in a set sequence against an imaginary attacker or attackers, armed and unarmed.

With this in mind the Karate-Ka should, through practise, not only understand his Kihon (basic) techniques but also be aware of the Bunkai (applications).

# KATA : *Formal Exercise*

The majority of time Kata is practised alone to enable the the Karate-Ka his own time to visualise how these techniques would be effective in reality, but constant practise with a partner is also a must, to ascertain distance and timing when applying Kihon applications. Courtesy is shown throughout Karate and is always made apparent when practising Kata by the Karate-Ka beginning and ending with a bow (Rei).

Listed below are the ten elements of Kata as taught by Sensei Kanazawa

1 **Yoi No Kisin** – the spirit of getting ready. The concentration of will and mind against the opponent as a preliminary to the movements of the Kata.

2 **Inyo** – the active and passive. Always keeping in mind both attack and defence.

3 **Chikara No Kyojaku** – the manner of using strength. The degree of power used for each movement and position in Kata.

4 **Waza No Kankyu** – the speed of movement. The speed used for each movement and position in Kata.

5 **Tai No Shinshuku** – the degree of expansion or contraction. The degree of expansion or contraction of the body in each movement and position in Kata.

6 **Kokyu** – breathing. Breath control related to the posture and movement in Kata.

7 **Tyakugan** – the aiming points. In Kata you must keep the purpose of the movement in mind.

8 **Kiai** – shouting. Shouting at set points in Kata to demonstrate the martial spirit.

9 **Keitai No Hoji** – correct positioning. Correct positioning in movement and stance.

10 **Zanshin** – remaining on guard. Remaining on guard at the completion of the Kata (i.e. back to "Yoi") until told to relax "Enoy".

For ease of reference photographs are laid out in sequence across each spread of pages.

To assist the Karate Ka in their performance of Kata throughout this section, directions have been illustrated by the arrow of the compass e.g.

# BASSAI SHO

Bassai Sho can be
attributed fairly
accurately to Master
Itosu.

Bassai have many
different forms in
various styles.
Using Bo in the
bunkai of this kata
requires strong
stance and blocking
techniques and the
use of hips.

# BASSAI SHO

(a) YOI

(b) YOI

(c) Side view

(d) Intermediate movement

2. Kokutsu Dachi
   Morote Koko Uke

2(a). Side view

3. Kokutsu Dachi
   Suihei Bo Dori

3(a). Side view

(e) Intermediate movement

(f) Side view

1. Kosa Dachi
   Jodan Haishu Awase
   Uke

1(a). Side view

3(b). Intermediate
      movement

3(c). Heisoku Dachi
      Haito Sukui Nage

3(d). Intermediate
      movement

---

*Section 2: Kumite – Bassai Sho*

# BASSAI SHO

4. Heisoku Dachi
   Gedan Tetsui Uchi

4(a). Intermediate
      movement

5. Kokutsu Dachi
   Morote Koko Uke

6. Kokutsu Dachi
   Suihei Do Dori

8. Kiba Dachi
   Tate Shuto Uke

8(a). Kiba Dachi
      Migi Chudan Zuki

9. Kiba Dachi
   Hidari Chudan Zuki

9(a). Intermediate
      movement

6(a). Intermediate movement

6(b). Heisoku Dachi Haito Koshi Gamae

7. Yoko Geri Keage Doji Haito Uchi

7(a). Intermediate movement

10. Kokutsu Dachi Manji Uke

10(a). Intermediate movement

11. Kokutsu Dachi Manji Uke

11(a). Intermediate movement

# BASSAI SHO

12. Kokutsu Dachi
Migi Chudan Shuto
Uke

13. Kokutsu Dachi
Hidari Chudan Shuto
Uke

14. Kokutsu Dachi
Migi Chudan Shuto
Uke

15. Kokutsu Dachi
Hidari Chudan Shuto
Uke

17(a). Intermediate
movement

17(b). Side view

18. Kokutsu Dachi
Ryowan Uchi Uke

18(a). Side view

*The Advanced Shotokan Karate Handbook*

15(a). Intermediate
movement

16. Zenkutsu Dachi
Gyaku Hanmi
Kaeshi Dori

16(a). Intermediate
movement

17. Gedan Kekomi
**KIAI**

19. Kokutsu Dachi
Jodan Ura Zuki

19(a). Side view

19(b). Ashi Barai Chudan
Doji Uke

19(c). Kiba Dachi
Koshi Gamae

---

*Section 2: Kumite – Bassai Sho*

# BASSAI SHO

20. Kiba Dachi
Sokumen Morote Zuki

20(a). Side view

20(b). Intermediate
movement

21. Kiba Dachi
Chudan Tetsui Uke

22(d). Kiba Dachi
Koshi Gamae

23. Kiba Dachi
Sokumen Morote
Zukl

23(a). Ashi Barai
Chudan Doji Uke

23(b). Kiba Dachi
Koshi Gamae

22. Zenkutsu Dachi
    Migi Chudan Oi Zuki
    **KIAI**

22(a). Intermediate
       movement

22(b). Ashi Barai
       Chudan Doji Uke

22(c). Front view

24. Kiba Dachi
    Sokumen Morote
    Zuki

24(a). Ashi Barai
       Chudan Doji Uke

24(b). Kiba Dachi
       Koshi Gamae

25. Kiba Dachi
Sokumen Morote Zuki

25(a). Intermediate
movement

25(b). Intermediate
movement

25(c). Intermediate
movement

27. Yoko Sashi Ashi

27(a). Intermediate
movement

27(b). Ura Ashigake
Jodan Shuto Doji
Uke

27(c). Intermediate
movement

25(d). Ura Ashigake
Jodan Doji Uke

25(e). Intermediate
movement

25(f). Intermediate
movement

26. Neko Ashi Dachi
Morote Hiki Otoshi

28. Neko Ashi Dachi
Morote Hiki Otoshi

28(a). Yame

28(b). Yame

# BASSAI SHO

**Application 1**

1(a)

1(b)

1(c)

**Application 2**

2(a)

2(b)

**Application 3**

3(a)

3(b)

3(c)

# BASSAI SHO

**Application 4**

4(a)

4(b)

4(c)

4(d)

4(e)

4(f)

4(g)

**Application 5**

5(a)

5(b)

5(c)

# BASSAI SHO

## Application 6

6(a)

6(b)

6(c)

## Application 7

7(a)

7(b)

**Application 8**

8(a)

8(b)

*Karate-do begins with courtesy and ends
with courtesy*

# CHINTE

Formerly called Shoin by Master Funakoshi, this kata of Chinese origin involves mainly circular movements which utilise the shoulders extensively. It also includes unusual open hand techniques such as Age-Empi (Upper Rising Elbow), Nihon Nukite (Two finger spearhand) Teisho (Palm Heel) Nakadaka Ippon-Ken (Middle finger one knuckle fist), and one kick.

As it is a kata which uses close range self defence techniques requiring less power it is popular with women.

# CHINTE

(a). YOI

(b). Intermediate
movement

(c). Intermediate
movement

(d). Intermediate
movement

1(c). Intermediate
movement

1(d). Intermediate
movement

2. Heisoku Dachi
Hidari Tetsui Uchi

2(a). Intermediate
movement

*The Advanced Shotokan Karate Handbook*

(e). Intermediate movement

1. Heisoku Dachi
   Migi Tetsui Uchi

1(a). Intermediate
      movement

1(b). Bring fist back
      left fist on top

3. Kiba Dachi
   Awase Shuto Age Uke

3(a). Front view

3(b). Intermediate
      movement

---

4. Fudo Dachi
   Tate Shuto Uke

4(a). Side view

5. Zenkutsu Dachi
   Tate Ken Gyaku Zuki

5(a). Side view

8. Fudo Dachi
   Migi Tate Shuto Uke

9. Zenkutsu Dachi
   Hidari Age Empi Uchi
   **\*KIAI\***

9(a). Front view

9(b). Intermediate
   movement

5(b). Intermediate
movement

6. Fudo Dachi
   Hidari Tate Shuto Uke

7. Zenkutsu Dachi
   Tate Ken Gyaku Zuki

7(a). Intermediate
movement

10. Kokutsu Dachi
    Hidari Chudan Shuto
    Uke

11. Kokutsu Dachi
    Migi Chudan Shuto
    Uke

12. Hidari Jodan Maegeri

12(a). Intermediate
movement

# CHINTE

13. Zenkutsu Dachi

14. Heisoku Dachi
Naiwan Sukui
Nage

14(a). Intermediate
movement

15. Heisoku Dachi
Gedan Tetsui Uchi

16(b). Front view

16(c). Intermediate
movement

16(d). Front view

16(e). Front view

*The Advanced Shotokan Karate Handbook*

15(a). Intermediate
movement

15(b). Intermediate
movement

16. Kiba Dachi
Morote Haito Barai

16(a). Intermediate
movement

17. Kiba Dachi
Morote Haito Barai

17(a). Front view

17(b). Intermediate
movement

18. Kiba Dachi
    Ryowan Uchi Uke

18(a). Front view

18(b). Intermediate
       movement

18(c). Intermediate view

20(a). Intermediate
       movement

21. Zenkutsu Dachi
    Ippon Ken Otoshi

21(a). Intermediate
       movement

22. Zenkutsu Dachi
    Nihon Nukite Uchi
    Uke

18(d). Intermediate
movement

19. Tsuru Ashi Dachi
Ryowan Gamae

19(a). Intermediate
movement

20. Zenkutsu Dachi
Ippon Ken Otoshi

23. Zenkutsu Dachi
Hidari Jodan Nihon
Nukite

23(a). Intermediate
movement

24. Zenkutsu Dachi
Hidari Nihon Nukite
Uchi Uke

# CHINTE

25. Zenkutsu Dachi
    Jodan Nihon Nukite

25(a). Intermediate
       movement

26. Fudo Dachi
    Chudan Teisho Uchi

26(a). Intermediate
       movement

29. Fudo Dachi
    Hasami Uchi
    (Naka Daka Ippon Ken)
    **KIAI**

29(a). Close up

29(b). Intermediate
       movement

30. Fudo Dachi
    Migi Tate Shuto Uke

27. Zenkutsu Dachi
Hidari Teisho Uchi

27(a). Front view

28. Zenkutsu Dachi
Ushiro Morote Ippon Ken
(Naka Daka Ippon Ken)

28(a). Intermediate
movement

31. Zenkutsu Dachi
Tate Ken Gyaku Zuki

31(a). Intermediate
movement

32. Fudo Dachi
Hidari Tate Shuto Uke

33. Zenkutsu Dachi
Tate Ken Gyaku Zuki

# CHINTE

34. Heisoku Dachi
   Tsutsumi Ken
   Pulling front foot back

34(a). Intermediate
   movement
   Jump

34(b). Jump

34(c). YOI

## Application 1

1(a)

1(b)

1(c)

1(d)

## Application 2

2(a)

2(b)

2(c)

**Application 3**

3(a)

3(b)

3(c)

**Application 4**

4(a)

4(b)

**Application 5**

5(a)

5(b)

5(c)

5(d)

# CHINTE

5(e)

5(f)

5(g)

## Application 6

6(a)

6(b)

# GOJUSHIHO DAI

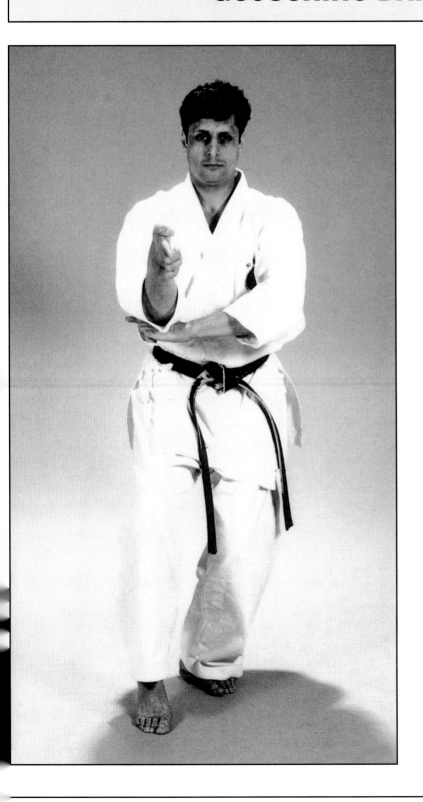

Formerly called Hotaku by Sensei Funakoshi because of its similarities to a woodpecker hitting a tree with its beak.

Gojushiho Dai has numerous advanced techniques which use Haito Uke and Washide (Eagle beak).

This kata also incorporates Keito nagashi uke into Ippon nukite.

# GOJUSHIHO DAI

(a). YOI

(b). Intermediate movement

1. Zenkutsu Dachi Uraken Gamae

1(a). Intermediate movement

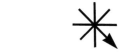

4. Zenkutsu Dachi Hidari Chudan Tate Shuto Uke

4(a). Zenkutsu Dachi Migi Chudan Gyaku Zuki

4(b). Zenkutsu Dachi Hidari Chudan Jun Zuki

4(c). Migi Mae Geri

2. Zenkutsu Dachi

2(a). Intermediate movement

3. Zenkutsu Dachi Heiko Tate Zuki

3(a). Intermediate movement

5. Zenkutsu Dachi Migi Chudan Gyaku Zuki

5(a). Intermediate movement

# GOJUSHIHO DAI

6. Zenkutsu Dachi
   Migi Chudan Tate
   Shuto Uke

6(a). Zenkutsu Dachi
   Hidari Chudan
   Gyaku Zuki

6(b). Zenkutsu Dachi
   Migii Chudan Jun
   Zuki

6(c). Hidari Mae Geri

8(b). Front view

9. Zenkutsu Dachi
   Koko Hiza Kuzushi

9(a). Front view

9(b) Intermediate
   movement

| 7. Zenkutsu Dachi Chudan Gyaku Zuki | 7(a). Intermediate movement | 8. Zenkutsu Dachi Age Empi | 8(a). Intermediate movement |

| 9(c). Front view | 10. Nekoashi Dachi Migi Keito Uke | 10(a). Front view |

# GOJUSHIHO DAI

11. Negashi Hidari Gedan
    Shuto Osae

11(a). Front view

12. Nekoashi Dachi
    Migi Ippon Nukite

12(a). Front view

13(b). Intermediate
    movement

13(c). Intermediate
    movement

14. Nekoashi Dachi
    Migi Keito Uke

15. Nekoashi Dachi
    Migi Keito Uke
    Nagashi Hidari Gedan
    Osae

12(b). Nekoashi Dachi
Hidari Ippon Nukite

12(c). Front view

13. Nekoashi Dachi
Migi Ippon Nukite

13(a). Front view

16. Nekoashi Dachi
Migi Ippon Nukite

16(a). Nekoashi Dachi
Hidari Ippon Nukite

17. Nekoashi Dachi
Migi Ippon Nukite

17(a). Intermediate
movement

# GOJUSHIHO DAI

18. Kiba Dachi
    Morote Kaishu Gedan
    Uke

19. Yoko Sashi Ashi

19(a).  Front view

19(b).  Jodan Koko Morote
        Uke

22(a).  Jodan Koko
        Morote Uke

23. Kiba Dachi Sokumen
    Gedan Morote Uke
    Otoshi Fumikomi

24. Nekoashi Dachi
    Migi Keito Uke

25. Nekoashi Dachi
    Keito Uke Nagashi
    Hidari Gedan Shuto
    Osae

**78**

*The Advanced Shotokan Karate Handbook*

20. Kiba Dachi
Sokumen Gedan
Morote Uke
Otoshi Fumikomi

20(a). Intermediate
movement

21. Kiba Dachi
Morote Kaishu Gedan
Uke

22. Yoko Sashi Ashi

26. Nekoashi Dachi
Migi Ippon Nukite

26(a). Nekoashi Dachi
Hidari Ippon
Nukite

27. Nekoashi Dachi
Migi Ippon Nukite

27(a). Intermediate
movement

---

28. Zenkutsu Dachi
    Migi Gedan Shuto
    Uchi

28(a). Intermediate
       movement

29. Zenkutsu Dachi
    Migi Uraken Uchi

30. Zenkutsu Dachi
    Hidari Gedan Shuto
    Uchi

33. Zenkutsu Dachi
    Washide Age Uchi

33(a). Hidari Mae Geri

33(b). Ippon Dachi
       Gedan Kosa Zuki

34. Zenkutsu Dachi
    Hidari Jodan Empi Uchi
    Ushiro Gedan Barai

30(a). Intermediate movement

31. Zenkutsu Dachi Hidari Uraken Uchi

31(a). Intermediate movement

32. Zenkutsu Dachi Washide Otoshi Uchi

34(a). Side view

34(b). Intermediate movement

35. Nekoashi Dachi Migi Keito Uke

36. Nekoashi Migi Keito Uke Negashi Hidari Gedan Shuto Osae

# GOJUSHIHO DAI

37. Nekoashi Dachi
Migi Ippon Nukite

37(a). Nekoashi Dachi
Hidari Ippon Nukite

38. Nekoashi Dachi
Migi Ippon Nukite

38(a). Intermediate
movement

41(a). Intermediate
movement

42. Kiba Dachi
Morote Keishu Gedan
Uke

43. Yoko Sashi Ashi

43(a). Intermediate
movement

39. Kiba Dachi
    Morote Kaishu Gedan
    Uke

40. Yoko Sashi Ashi

40(a). Ippon Dachi Chudan
       Tate Shuto Uke
       Fumikomi

41. Kiba Dachi Tate Shihon
    Nukite Yoko Hari Empi

43(b). Ippon Dachi
       Chudan Tate Shuto
       Uke Fumikomi

44. Kiba Dachi
    Tate Shihon Nukite
    Yoko Hari Empi

44(a). Intermediate
       movement

# GOJUSHIHO DAI

45. Zenkutsu Dachi
Jodan Uraken Gamae

45(a). Intermediate
movement

46. Kiba Dachi
Hidari Chudan Tetsui
Uchi

47. Zenkutsu Dachi
Migi Chudan Oi Zuki
**\*KIAI\***

50. Zenkutsu Dachi
Suihei Hiji Uchi

50(a). Front view

50(b). Intermediate
movement
Stepping forward

50(c). Intermediate
movement

*The Advanced Shotokan Karate Handbook*

48. Shizentai
    Suihei Hiji Gamae

48(a). Front view

48(b). Shizentai Ushiro
       Tetsui Hasami Uchi

49. Shizentai
    Suihei Hiji Gamae

51. Nekoashi Dachi
    Gedan Shuto
    Negashi Uke

52. Nekoashi Dachi
    Morote Keito Uke

52(a). Front view

52(b). Nekoashi Dachi
       Morote Gedan
       Ippon Nukite
       *KIAI*

52(c). Angle view

53. Nekoashi Dachi
    Morote Keito Uke

53(a). Front view

53(b). Intermediate
       movement

54. Nekoashi Dachi
    Migi Keito Uke

54(a). Intermediate
       movement

54(b). YAME

**Application 1**

(a)

1(b)

**Application 2**

(a)

2(b)

**Application 3**

(a)

3(b)

# GOJUSHIHO DAI

**Application 4**

4(a)

4(b)

4(c)

4(d)

**Application 5**

5(a)

5(b)

5(c)

5(d)

(e)

## Application 6

a)

6(b)

6(c)

6(d)

6(e)

6(f)

# GOJUSHIHO SHO

Previously called Hotaku by Sensei Funakoshi as mentioned in Gojushiho Dai, this kata is the most advanced from the school of Itosu.

It contains numerous hand techniques, Gedan morote kaishu uke and Ushiro Tetsui Hasami Uchi among them. This kata offers an abundance of easy disengagements through to strong striking counter attacks.

# GOJUSHIHO SHO

(a). YOI

(b). Intermediate movement

1. Zenkutsu Dachi Migi Uraken Uchi

1(a). Intermediate movement

4. Zenkutsu Dachi Hidari Chudan Tate Shuto Uke

4(a). Zenkutsu Dachi Migi Chudan Gyaku Zuki

4(b). Zenkutsu Dachi Hidari Chudan Zuki

4(c). Migi Mae Geri

2. Kokutsu Dachi
   Kakiwake Uke

2(a). Intermediate
   movement

3. Kokutsu Dachi
   Kakiwake Uke

3(a). Intermediate
   movement

5. Zenkutsu Dachi
   Migi Chudan Oi Zuki

5(a). Intermediate
   movement

# GOJUSHIHO SHO

6. Zenkutsu Dachi
   Migi ChudanTate
   Shuto Uke

6(a). Zenkutsu Dachi
   Hidari Chudan
   Gyaku Zuki

6(b). Zenkutsu Dachi
   Migi Chudan Zuki

6(c). Hidari Mae Geri

9. Kokutsu Dachi
   Ryu Un No Uke

9(a). Side view

10. Kokutsu Dachi
   Kaishu Kosa Gamae

10(a). Side view

*The Advanced Shotokan Karate Handbook*

7. Zenkutsu Dachi
   Hidari Chudan Oi Zuki

7(a). Intermediate
      movement

8. Zenkutsu Dachi
   Jodan Age Empi

8(a). Intermediate
      movement

11. Zenkutsu Dachi
    Migi Shihon Nukite

11(a). Angle view

11(b). Intermediate
       movement

11(c). Angle view

12. Zenkutsu Dachi
Migi Shihon Nukite

12(a). Angle view

12(b). Intermediate
movement

13. Kokutsu Dachi
Ryu Un No Uke

17. Kiba Dachi
Morote Kaishu Gedan
Uke

17(a). Intermediate
movement

17(b). Fumikomi

17(c). Front view

14. Kokutsu Dachi
    Kaishu Kosa Uke

15. Zenkutsu Dachi
    Migi Shihon Nukite

15(a). Zenkutsu Dachi
       Hidari Shihon
       Nukite

16. Zenkutsu Dachi
    Migi Shihon Nukite

18. Kiba Dachi
    Hidari Koshi Gamae

18(a). Front view

# GOJUSHIHO SHO

19. Kiba Dachi
    Morote Kaishu
    Gedan Uke

19(a). Intermediate
       movement

19(b). Front view

19(c). Fumikomi

22. Kokutsu Dachi
    Kaishu Kosa Uke

23. Zenkutsu Dachi
    Migi Shihon Nukite

23(a). Zenkutsu Dachi
       Hidari Shihon
       Nukite

24. Zenkutsu Dachi
    Migi Shihon Nukite

*The Advanced Shotokan Karate Handbook*

19(d). Front view

20. Kiba Dachi
    Migi Koshi Gamae

20(a). Intermediate
       movement

21. Kokutsu Dachi
    Ryu Un No Uke

24(a). Intermediate
       movement

25. Zenkutsu Dachi
    Migi Jodan Shuto
    Uchi

25(a). Intermediate
       movement

26. Zenkutsu Dachi
    Migi Jodan Shuto Uke

26(a). Intermediate
       movement

27. Zenkutsu Dachi
    Hidari Shuto Uchi

27(a). Intermediate
       movement

29(b). Kosa Dachi
       Migi Nagashi Uke
       Hidari Otoshi Zuki

30. Zenkutsu Dachi
    Ushiro Gedan Barai

30(a). Intermediate
       movement

31. Kokutsu Dachi
    Ryu Un No Uke

*The Advanced Shotokan Karate Handbook*

28. Zenkutsu Dachi
    Hidari Jodan Shuto
    Uchi

28(a). Intermediate
       movement

29. Zenkutsu Dachi
    Gyaku Hanmi Migi
    Chudan Uchi Uke

29(a). Migi Mae Geri

32. Kokutsu Dachi
    Kaishu Kosa Uke

33. Zenkutsu Dachi
    Migi Shihon Nukite

33(a). Zenkutsu Dachi
       Hidari Shihon
       Nukite

# GOJUSHIHO SHO

34. Zenkutsu Dachi
    Migi Shihon Nukite

34(a). Intermediate
       movement

35. Kiba Dachi
    Morote Kaishu
    Gedan Uke

35(a). Intermediate
       movement
       Step over

37(a). Intermediate
       movement
       Stepping over

37(b). Intermediate
       movement

37(c). Fumikomi

37(d). Intermediate
       movement

*The Advanced Shotokan Karate Handbook*

35(b). Intermediate movement

35(c) Fumikomi

36. Kiba Dachi
Migi Chudan Zuki

37. Kiba Dachi
Morote Kaishu Gedan Uke

38. Kiba Dachi
Migi Chudan Zuki

38(a). Intermediate movement

39. Zenkutsu Dachi
Migi Uraken Uchi

39(a). Kiba Dachi
Hidari Chudan Tetsui Uchi

# GOJUSHIHO SHO

40. Zenkutsu Dachi
    Migi Chudan Oi Zuki
    **\*KIAI\***

40(a). Shizentai
       Ryo Wan Zenpo
       Nobashi

40(b). Front view

40(c). Ushiro Tetsui
       Hasami Uchi

43. Neko Ashi Dachi
    Ryo Kaishu Gamae

44. Neko Ashi Dachi
    Morote Keito Uke

44(a). Front view

45. Neko Ashi Dachi
    Morote Seiryuto Uchi
    **\*KIAI\***

*The Advanced Shotokan Karate Handbook*

41. Shizentai
Ryo Goshi Gamae

42. Zenkutsu Dachi
Ryo Goshi Gamae

42(a). Intermediate
movement

42(b). Front view

45(a). Front view

45(b). Intermediate
movement

46. Kokutsu Dachi
Ryu Un No Uke

46(a). YAME

# GOJUSHIHO SHO

**Application 1**

1(a)

1(b)

1(c)

1(d)

1(e)

1(f)

1(g)

1(h)

## Application 2

2(a)

2(b)

2(c)

2(d)

# GOJUSHIHO SHO

2(e)

2(f)

2(g)

2(h)

2(i)

2(j)

2(k)

**Application 3**

3(a)

3(b)

3(c)

3(d)

3(e)

# KANKU SHO

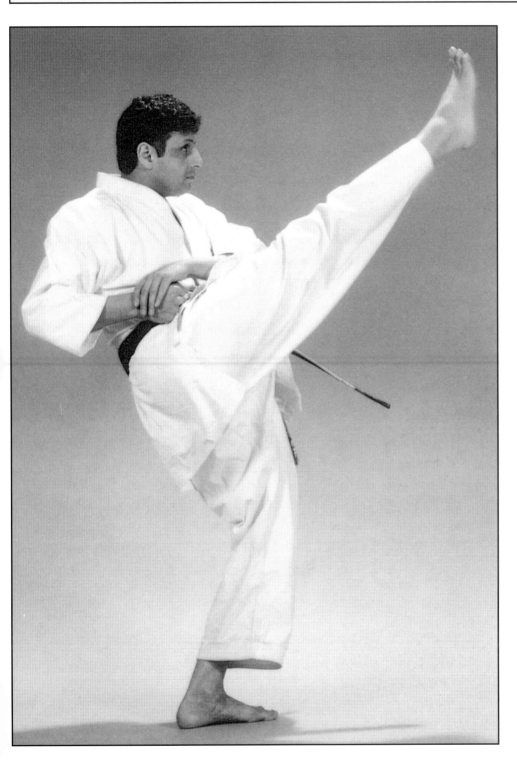

Kanku Sho is also known as Kushanku and was created by Sensei Itosu.

Following Kanku Dai this kata starts with Morote Uke from three directions. It demands a higher technical understanding, although it is perhaps not as impressive as the start in Kanku Dai.

This kata also incorporates two jumping techniques, the first to avoid Ashi-barai or a weapon such as a Bo.

Sensei Itosu's most senior student, Chibana, practised and taught this kata, passing on his knowledge to his students.

# KANKU SHO

(a). YOI

(b). Intermediate movement

1. Kokutsu Dachi Migi Chudan Morote Uke

1(a). Intermediate movement

3(b). Zenkutsu Dachi Migi Chudan Oi Zuki

4. Zenkutsu Dachi Hineri Kaeshi

4(a). Zenkutsu Dachi Hidari Chudan Oi Zuki

5. Zenkutsu Dachi Hineri Kaeshi

*The Advanced Shotokan Karate Handbook*

2. Kokutsu Dachi Migi Chudan Morote Uke

2(a). Intermediate movement

3. Kokutsu Dachi Hidari Chudan Morote Uke

3(a). Intermediate movement

6. Zenkutsu Dachi Migi Chudan Oi Zuki **\*KIAI\***

6(a). Intermediate movement

6(b). Side view

6(c). Intermediate movement

7. Moto Dachi
   Soete Kake Dori

7(a). Side view

7(b). Tsukami Dori
   Migi Maegeri

7(c). Side view

8(b). Intermediate
   movement

8(c). Side view

9. Zenkutsu Dachi
   Chudan Uchi Uke

9(a). Side view

7(d). Intermediate movement
Hidari Chudan Osai
Uke

7(e). Side view

8. Kosa Dachi
Chudan Uraken Uchi

8(a). Side view

9(b). Zenkutsu Dachi
Chudan Gyaku Zuki

9(c). Side view

10. Zenkutsu Dachi
    Chudan Jun Zuki

10(a).  Side view

10(b).  Intermediate
        movement

10(c).  Intermediate
        movement

12(b).  Intermediate
        movement

12(c).  Intermediate
        movement

13.  Moto Dachi
     Soete Kake Dori

13(a). Tsukami Dori
       Maegeri

11. Kokutsu Dachi
Migi Ken Uchi Uke
Hidari Ken Gedan
Barai

11(a). Intermediate
movement

12. Hidari Shizentai
Gedan Gamae

12(a). Intermediate
movement

13(b). Side view

13(c). Intermediate
movement

13(d). Intermediate
movement
Hidari Chudan
Osai Uke

14. Kosa Dachi
    Uraken Uchi

14(a). Intermediate
       movement

15. Zenkutsu Dachi
    Chudan Uchi Uke

15(a). Zenkutsu Dachi
       Chudan Gyaku Zuki

18. Hidari Shizentai
    Gedan Gamae

18(a). Intermediate
       movement

19. Kokutsu Dachi
    Manji Uke

19(a). Side view

16. Zenkutsu Dachi
    Chudan Jun Zuki

16(a). Intermediate
    movement

17. Kokutsu Dachi
    Migi Ken Uchi Uke
    Hidari Ken Gedan Barai

17(a). Intermediate
    movement

19(b). Kokutsu Dachi
    Hidari Chudan Ude
    Uke

19(c). Side view

20. Kiba Dachi
Morote Zuki

20(a). Front view

20(b). Intermediate
movement

21. Kokutsu Dachi
Manji Uke

22(c). Intermediate
movement

22(d). Front view

23. Kokutsu Dachi
Bo Uke

23(a). Front view

21(a). Kokutsu Dachi
Migi Chudan Ude
Uke

22. Kiba Dachi
Morote Zuki

22(a). Intermediate
movement

22(b). Front view

24. Kokutsu Dachi
Sliding forward
Bo Dori Zuki Otoshi

24(a). Front view

24(b). Intermediate
movement

24(c). Intermediate
movement
**\*KIAI\***

# KANKU SHO

25. Kokutsu Dachi
Migi Chudan Shuto
Uke

25(a). Intermediate
movement

25(b). Hidari Yoko Keage
Doji Uraken Uchi

26. Zenkutsu Dachi
Migi Mae Empi

27(a). Intermediate
movement

27(b). Intermediate
movement

28. Moto Dachi
Soete Kake Dori

28(a). Tsukami Dori
Migi Maegeri

*The Advanced Shotokan Karate Handbook*

# KANKU SHO

26(a). Intermediate movement

26(b). Intermediate movement

26(c). Migi Yoko Keage Doji Uraken Uchi

27. Zenkutsu Dachi Hidari Mae Empi

28(b). Chudan Osai Uke

29. Kosa Dachi Uraken Uchi

30. Zenkutsu Dachi Chudan Uchi Uke

30(a). Zenkutsu Dachi Chudan Gyaku Zuki

*Section 2: Kumite – Kanku Sho*

**123**

31. Zenkutsu Dachi
    Chudan Jun Zuki

31(a). Intermediate
       movement

31(b). Side view

31(c). Intermediate
       movement

32(d). Jodan Tobi Mika
       Zuki Geri

32(e). Intermediate
       movement

32(f). Intermediate
       movement

32(g). Front view

32. Zenkutsu Dachi
    Jodan Haishu Uke

32(a).  Side view

32(b).  Intermediate
        movement

32(c).  Intermediate
        movement

33. Ryote Fuse

33(a). Front view

33(b). Intermediate movement

33(c). Side view

35(a). Side view

35(b). Intermediate movement

36. Zenkutsu Dachi Hidari Chudan Uchi Uke

37. Zenkutsu Dachi Migi Chudan Oi Zuki

33(d). Side view

34. Kokutsu Dachi
    Morote Gedan Shuto
    Uke

34(a). Side view

35. Kokutsu Dachi
    Migi Chudan Shuto
    Uke

37(a). Intermediate
       movement

38. Zenkutsu Dachi
    Migi Chudan Uchi Uke

39. Zenkutsu Dachi
    Hidari Chudan Oi Zuki

39(a). **YAME**

# KANKU SHO

**Application 1**

1(a)

1(b)

1(c)

1(d)

1(e)

1(f)

*The Advanced Shotokan Karate Handbook*

1(g)

**Application 2**

2(a)

2(b)

2(c)

2(d)

# KANKU SHO

2(e)

2(f)

2(g)

2(h)

2(i)

2(j)

2(k)

2(l)

**Application 3**

3(a)

3(b)

3(c)

**Application 4**

4(a)

4(b)

4(c)

4(d)

4(e)

4(f)

# MEIKYO

Meikyo was previously known as ROHAI, meaning 'a brightly polished mirror'. It was later renamed Meikyo by Sensei Funakoshi. It is in this kata that we see the introduction of SANAKU-TOBI, the triangualar jump, as well as some close fighting techniques.

(a). YOI

(b). Intermediate
movement

(c). Intermediate
movement

(d). Intermediate
movement

2. Kiba Dachi
Joshin Gamae

2(a). Intermediate
movement

3. Zenkutsu Dachi
Hidari Gedan Barai

4. Zenkutsu Dachi
Migi Chudan Oi Zuki

(e). Intermediate
movement

1. Kiba Dachi
Ryo Goshi Gamae

1(a). Intermediate
movement

1(b). Intermediate
movement

4(a). Intermediate
movement

5. Zenkutsu Dachi
Migi Gedan Barai

6. Zenkutsu Dachi
   Hidari Chudan Oi Zuki

6(a). Intermediate
   movement

6(b). Intermediate
   movement

7. Kokutsu Dachi
   Morote Jo Uke
   Bo block

9(a). Side view

9(b). Intermediate
   movement

9(c). Intermediate
   movement

9(d). Intermediate
   movement

7(a). Side view

8. Jo Zukami

8(a). Side view

9. Turning

10. Kiba Dachi
    Ryo Goshi Gamae

11. Zenkutsu Dachi
    Hidari Chudan Uchi
    Uke

12. Zenkutsu Dachi
    Migi Chudan Oi Zuki

12(a). Intermediate
      movement

13. Zenkutsu Dachi
Migi Chudan Uchi Uke

14. Zenkutsu IDachi
Hidari Chudan Oi Zuki

14(a). Intermediate
movement

14(b). Intermediate
movement

17(b). Intermediate
movement

17(c). Intermediate
movement

18. Kiba Dachi
Ryo Goshi Gamae

18(a). Intermediate
movement

15. Kokutsu Dachi
    Morote Jo Uke

16. Jo Zukami

17. Intermediate
    movement

17(a). Back view

19. Zenkutsu Dachi
    Hidari Jodan Age Uke

20. Zenkutsu Dachi
    Migi Chudan Oi Zuki

20(a). Intermediate
       movement

21. Zenkutsu Dachi
    Migi Jodan Age Uke

22. Zenkutsu Dachi
Hidari Chudan Oi Zuki

22(a). Intermediate
movement

23. Kiba Dachi
Hidari Chudan Tetsui
Uke

24. Mikazuki Geri
*KIAI*

26(a). Intermediate
movement

27. Kokutsu Dachi
Morote Haiwan Uke

27(a). Intermediate
movement

28. Zenkutsu Dachi
Ryo Wan Gamae

24(a). Intermediate
movement

25. Kokutsu Dachi
Ryo Wan Gamae

25(a). Intermediate
movement

26. Kokutsu Dachi
Morote Haiwan Uke

28(a). Intermediate
movement

29. Kokutsu Dachi
Ryowan Uchi Uke

29(a). Kokutsu Dachi
Morote Kizami Ura
Zuki

30. Intermediate movement

30(a). Intermediate movement

31. Kokutsu Dachi
Hidari Jodan Age Uke

32. Sankaku Tobi Empi Uchi
**\*KIAI\***

33. Kokutsu Dachi
Migi Chudan Shuto
Uke

34. Kokutsu Dachi
Migi Chudan Shuto
Uke

34(a). YAME

# MEIKYO

**Application 1**

1(a)

1(b)

1(c)

1(d)

1(e)

1(f)

1(g)

**Application 2**

2(a)

2(b)

2(c)

# MEIKYO

**Application 3**

3(a)

3(b)

3(c)

3(d)

3(e)

3(f)

3(g)

3(h)

3(i)

**Application 4**

4(a)

4(b)

4(c)

4(d)

# NIJUSHIHO

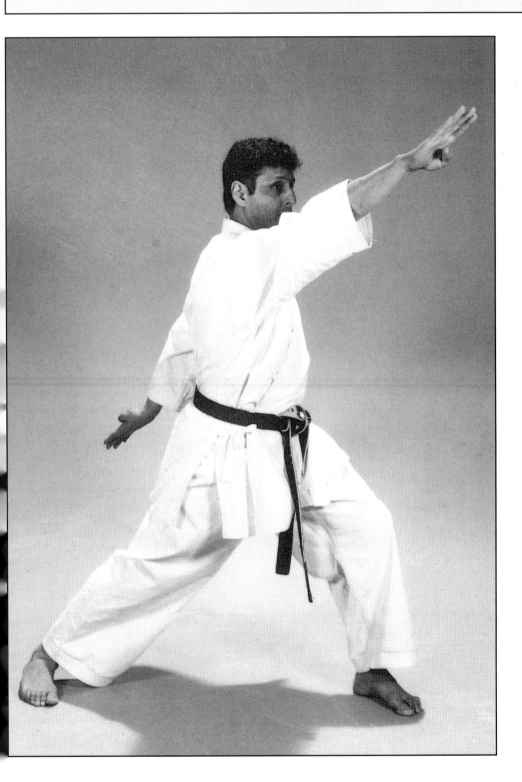

Formerly known as Niseishi, Nijushiho literally means twenty-four steps.

This is a kata practised in many styles, some of its techniques are similar to Unsu, Sochin and others. It could belong to the Aragaki group.

Osae-Uke the first technique in the kata is blocking a Chudan punch in Kokutsu-Dachi. Remaining in the same stance, counter with Gyaku-zuki, slide forward, and finish with Empi-Uchi.

These sequences are executed at the same time throughout some kata movements.

(a). YOI

(b). Intermediate
movement
sliding backwards

1. Kokutsu Dachi
Ryusui No Kamae

1(a). Intermediate
movement

2(b). Intermediate
movement

2(c). Intermediate
movement

3. Sanchin Dachi
Ryo Goshi Gamae

3(a). Front view

1(b). Kokutsu Dachi
Ryusui Zuki
Sliding forward

1(c). Intermediate
movement

2. Hidari Shizentai
Empi Uchi

2(a). Intermediate
movement

3(b). Sanchin Dachi
Awase Zuki

3(c). Front view

3(d). Muso Uke
Hasami Uke Hiza
Gamae

3(e). Front view

3(f). Intermediate movement

3(g). Front view

4. Zenkutsu Dachi Kakiwake Uke

4(a). Front view

5(b). Intermediate movement

5(c). Front view

6. Kiba Dachi Sokumen Tate Shuto Uke

6(a). Front view

4(b). Intermediate movement

4(c). Zenkutsu Hidari Jodan Age Uke

5. Zenkutsu Dachi Migi Tate Empi

5(a). Side view

6(b). Migi ken Migi Koshi Yoko Geri Kekomi

7. Kiba Dachi Hidari Chudan Zuki

7(a). Intermediate movement

7(b). Front view

8. Kiba Dachi
   Hidari Chudan Tate
   Shuto Uke

8(a). Hidari Ken
   Hidari Koshi Yoko
   Geri Kekomi

9. Kiba Dachi
   Migi Chudan Zuki

9(a). Intermediate
   movement

11. Turning
   Zenkutsu Dachi
   Migi Jodan Haito Uchi
   Hidari Gedan Haito Uke

12. Heisoku Dachi
   Hidari Haishu Age Uchi
   **\*KIAI\***

12(a). Intermediate
   movement

12(b). Zenkutsu Dachi
   Koko Hiza Kuzushi

9(b). Migi Chudan
Kake Uke

9(c). Intermediate
movement

9(d). Front view

10. Zenkutsu Dachi
Teisho Awase Zuki

12(c). Intermediate
movement

13. Fudo Dachi
Gedan Awasi Zuki

13(a). Intermediate
movement

14. Kokutsu Dachi
Chudan Haishu Uke

15. Kiba Dachi
    Sokumen Tate Empi

15(a). Kiba Dachi
    Sokumen Soto Uke
    Gedan Zuki

16. Kiba Dachi
    Sokumen Migi Gedan
    Barai

16(a). Intermediate
    movement

18(a). Front view

18(b). Intermediate
    movement

19. Kokutsu Dachi
    Hidari Chudan Haishu
    Uke

20. Kiba Dachi
    Hidari Tate Empi

17. Kokutsu Dachi
    Hidari Haishu Uke

17(a). Kiba Dachi
       Mae Empi

17(b). Front view

18. Kiba Dachi
    Migi Gedan Barai
    Hidari Soete

20(a). Kiba Dachi
       Migi Soto Uke
       Hidari Gedan Zuki

21. Kiba Dachi
    Migi Gedan Barai

21(a). Turning
       Intermediate
       movement

21(b). Intermediate
       movement

22. Sanchin Dachi
    Ryo Goshi Gamae

23. Sanchin Dachi
    Awase Zuki
    **\*KIAI\***

23(a). Intermediate
       movement

23(b). Intermediate
       movement

23(c).  Sanchin Dachi
        Mawashi Kake Uke

24.  Migi Sanchin Dachi
     Awase Teisho Zuki

24(a).  **YAME**

# NIJUSHIHO

**Application 1**

1(a)

1(b)

1(c)

1(d)

1(e)

**Application 2**

2(a)

2(b)

2(c)

2(d)

2(e)

2(f)

2(g)

2(h)

## Application 3

3(a)

3(b)

## Application 4

4(a)

4(b)

(c)

4(d)

**Application 5**

(a)

5(b)

(c)

**Application 6**

6(a)

6(b)

6(c)

6(d)

6(e)

6(f)

6(g)

## Application 7

(a)

7(b)

(c)

7(d)

7(e)

**Application 8**

8(a)

8(b)

8(c)

**Application 9**

9(a)

9(b)

9(c)

9(d)

9(e)

9(f)

# NIJUSHIHO

9(g)

9(h)

9(i)

# SOCHIN

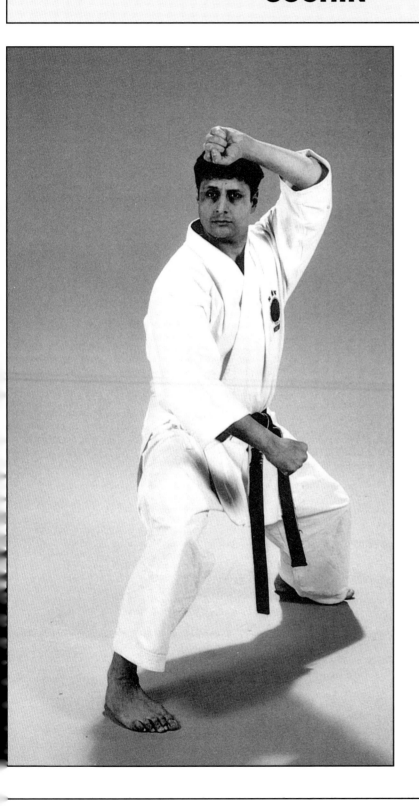

Sochin was previously known as HAKKO. Sochin means 'rooted' and derives from Sochin-Dachi (rooted stance) or Fudo Dachi, an intermediate position between Kiba Dachi and Zenkutsu Dachi. It is strengthened vertically and horizontally and gives the impression of being rooted to the spot, which is a distinguishing feature in this kata. The stance is strong and powerful and creates a sturdy base for resisting attacks. Here we see the introduction of MUSO GAMAE as the opening technique.

# SOCHIN

(a). YOI

(b). Intermediate movement

(c). Intermediate movement

1. Sochin Dachi Muso Gamae

4(a). Intermediate movement

4(b). Intermediate movement

5. Kokutsu Dachi Manji Gamae

5(a). Intermediate movement

*The Advanced Shotokan Karate Handbook*

1(b).  Intermediate
        movement

2.  Sochin Dachi
    Migi Chudan Tate
    Shuto Uke

3.  Sochin Dachi
    Hidari Chudan Zuki

4.  Sochin Dachi
    Migi Chudan Gyaku Zuki

6.  Sochin Dachi
    Muso Gamae

6(a).  Intermediate
        movement

7.  Sochin Dachi
    Migi Chudan Tate
    Shuto Uke

8.  Sochin Dachi
    Hidari Chudan Zuki

# SOCHIN

9. Sochin Dachi
Migi Chudan Gyaku
Zuki

9(a). Intermediate
movement

10. Kokutsu Dachi
Manji Gamae

10(a). Intermediate
movement

14. Sochin Dachi
Migi Chudan Gyaku
Zuki

14(a). Intermediate
movement

15. Hidari Yoko Geri Keage
Uraken Uchi

16. Sochin Dachi
Migi Empi Uchi

11. Sochin Dachi
    Muso Gamae

11(a). Intermediate
    movement

12. Sochin Dachi
    Migi Chudan Tate
    Shuto Uke

13. Sochin Dachi
    Hidari Chudan Zuki

16(a). Intermediate
    movement

6(b). Intermediate
    movement

17. Hidari Yoko Geri Keage
    Uraken Uchi

# SOCHIN

18. Sochin Dachi
    Hidari Empi Uchi

18(a). Intermediate
    movement

19. Kokutsu Dachi
    Migi Chudan Shuto Uke

20. Kokutsu Dachi
    Hidari Chudan Shuto
    Uke

24. Kokutsu Dachi
    Hidari Chudan Shuto
    Uke

25. Sliding forward
    Hidari Osae Uke
    Migi Nukite

25(a). Side view

26. Hidari Mae Geri

21. Kokutsu Dachi
Hidari Chudan Shuto
Uke

22. Kokutsu Dachi
Migi Chudan Shuto
Uke

22(a). Intermediate
movement

23. Kokutsu Dachi
Migi Chudan Shuto
Uke

26(a). Side view

27. Migi Jodan Mae Geri
Migi Negashi Uke
Hidari Uraken Uchi

27(a). Side view

# SOCHIN

28. Sochin Dachi
Hidari Negashi Uke
Migi Uraken Uchi
**\*KIAI\***

28(a).  Side view

29.  Mikazuki Geri

30. Sochin Dachi
Muso Gamae

33. Sochin Dachi
Migi Chudan Uchi Uke

34. Sochin Dachi
Hidari Chudan Oi Zuki

34(a).  Intermediate
movement

35. Sochin Dachi
Hidari Chudan Uchi
Uke

*The Advanced Shotokan Karate Handbook*

30(a). Intermediate movement

31. Sochin Dachi Hidari Chudan Uchi Uke

32. Sochin Dachi Migi Chudan Oi Zuki

32(a). Intermediate movement

35(a). Intermediate movement

36. Sochin Dachi Gyaku Hanmi Migi Chudan Uchi Uke

37. Migi Jodan Mae Geri

38. Sochin Dachi Hidari Yumi Zuki

# SOCHIN

39. Sochin Dachi
Migi Chudan Gyaku
Zuki

40. Sochin Dachi
Hidari Chudan Zuki
**\*KIAI\***

40(a).  YAME

**Application 1**

1(a)

1(b)

1(c)

1(d)

1(e)

1(f)

# SOCHIN

**Application 2**

2(a)

2(b)

2(c)

2(d)

2(e)

**180**

*The Advanced Shotokan Karate Handbook*

**Application 3**

3(a)

3(b)

3(c)

3(d)

3(e)

3(f)

*Always be ready to release your mind*

# TEKKI NIDAN

The original name of this kata was Naihanchi. It was renamed Tekki by Sensei Funakoshi.

Tekki katas are performed horizontally because according to Chinese Martial Arts history, they would be used for fighting in a boat or with your back against a wall.

Sensei Itosu created Tekki Nidan and Tekki Sandan, using Tekki Shodan as its foundation.

These katas should be practised by Nidans and above.

# TEKKI NIDAN

(a). YOI

(b). Intermediate
movement

1. Kosa Dachi
Ryo Hiji Harai Age

1(a). Intermediate
movement
Raising right leg

5. Heisoku Dachi
Ryo Hiji Harai Age

5(a). Intermediate
movement
Raising left leg

5(b). Intermediate
movement

6. Kiba Dachi
Sokumen Uke
Doji Fumikomi

*The Advanced Shotokan Karate Handbook*

2. Kiba Dachi
   Sokumen Ukc Doji
   Fumikomi

3. Kosa Dachi
   Gedan Soto Ude Uke

4. Kiba Dachi
   Sokumen Gedan
   Uchi Ude Uke

4(a). Intermediate
      movement

7. Kosa Dachi
   Gedan Soto Ude Uke

8. Kiba Dachi
   Sokumen Gedan
   Uchi Ude Uke

9. Kiba Dachi
   Koshi Gamae

# TEKKI NIDAN

10. Kiba Dachi
    Sokumen Uke

10(a). Intermediate
       movement

10(b). Intermediate
       movement
       Raising right leg

11. Kiba Dachi
    Mae Empi Doji
    Fumikomi

14. Raising right leg

15. Kiba Dachi
    Hidari Uchi Uke
    Doji Fumikomi

15(a). Intermediate
       movement

16. Kiba Dachi
    Migi Jodan Nagashi
    Uke

*The Advanced Shotokan Karate Handbook*

11(a). Intermediate movement

12. Kiba Dachi Migi Tate Shuto Uke

13. Kiba Dachi Hidari Kagi Zuki

13(a). Intermediate movement Yoko Sashi Ashi

17. Kiba Dachi Migi Jodan Ura Zuki *KIAI*

18. Kiba Dachi Koshi Gamae

19. Kiba Dachi Sokumen Uke

19(a). Intermediate movement

20. Intermediate
    movement
    Raising left leg

21. Kiba Dachi
    Mae Empi Doji
    Fumikomi

21(a). Intermediate
       movement

22. Kiba Dachi
    Hidari Tate Shuto Uke

25(a). Intermediate
       movement

26. Kiba Dachi
    Hidari Jodan Nagashi
    Uke

27. Kiba Dachi
    Hidari Jodan Ura Zuki
    **\*KIAI\***

27(a). YAME

23. Kiba Dachi
    Migi Kagi Zuki

23(a). Intermediate
    movement

24. Raising left leg

25. Kiba Dachi
    Migi Uchi Uke
    Doji Fumikomi

# TEKKI NIDAN

**Application 1**

1(a)

1(b)

1(c)

1(d)

1(e)

**Application 2**

2(a)

2(b)

# TEKKI NIDAN

**Application 3**

3(a)

3(b)

3(c)

3(d)

3(e)

# TEKKI SANDAN

The original name of this kata was Naihanchi but it was renamed Tekki by Sensei Funakoshi.

Tekki katas are performed horizontally because according to Chinese Martial Arts history they would be used for fighting in a boat or with the back against a wall.

Sensei Itosu created Tekki Nidan and Tekki Sandan using Tekki Shodan as its foundation.

These katas should be practised by Nidans and above.

# TEKKI SANDAN

(a). YOI

(b). Intermediate
movement

1. Kiba Dachi
Hidari Chudan
Uchi Uke

1(a). Intermediate
movement

6. Kiba Dachi
Ryusui No Kamae

7. Kiba Dachi
Migi Chudan Choku
Zuki

8. Kiba Dachi
Soesho Kaeshi
Ude

9. Kosa Dachi
Yoko Sashi Ashi

2. Kiba Dachi
   Kosa Uke

3. Yoko Ude Hasami

4. Kiba Dachi
   Migi Jodan Nagashi
   Uke

5. Kiba Dachi
   Migi Jodan Ura Zuki

10. Kiba Dachi
    Migi Sokumen
    Gedan Uchi Ude Uke

10(a). Intermediate
       movement

10(b). Intermediate
       movement

11. Kiba Dachi
    Migi Sokumen Tettsui
    Otoshi Uchi

---

# TEKKI SANDAN

12. Kiba Dachi
    Soesho Hikite

13. Kiba Dachi
    Migi Chudan Zuki

14. Kiba Dachi
    Kosa Uke

15. Kiba Dachi
    Kosa Uke

18. Raising left leg

19. Kiba Dachi
    Uraken Gamae Doji
    Fumikomi

20. Kiba Dachi
    Yoko Ude Hasami

21. Kiba Dachi
    Hidari Jodan Negashi
    Uke

16. Kiba Dachi
    Hidari Jodan
    Negashi Uke
    Migi Gedan Zuki

17. Kiba Dachi
    Hidari Jodan Ura Zuki
    *KIAI*

17(a). Intermediate
       movement

17(b). Kosa Dachi
       Yoko Sashi Ashi

22. Kiba Dachi
    Hidari Jodan
    Ura Zuki

23. Kiba Dachi
    Ryusui No Kamae

24. Kiba Dachi
    Hidari Chudan Zuki

25. Kiba Dachi
    Soesho Kaeshi Ude

25(a). Yoko Sashi Ashi

26. Kiba Dachi
    Sokumen Gedan
    Uchi Hidari Ude Uke

26(a). Intermediate
       movement

29(a). Intermediate
       movement

30. Kiba Dachi
    Migi Tate Shuto Uke

31. Kiba Dachi
    Hidari Kagi Zuki

31(a). Yoko Sashi Ashi

26(b). Intermediate
movement

27. Kiba Dachi
Hidari Sokumen
Tettsui Otoshi Uchi

28. Kiba Dachi
Soesho Hikite

29. Kiba Dachi
Hidari Chudan Zuki

32. Raising right leg

33. Kiba Dachi
Hidari Chudan Uchi
Uke Doji Fumikomi

34. Kiba Dachi
Kosa Uke

# TEKKI SANDAN

35. Kiba Dachi
    Migi Jodan Negashi
    Uke
    Hidari Gedan Zuki

36. Kiba Dachi
    Migi Jodan Ura Zuki
    **\*KIAI\***

36(a).  YAME

**Application 1**

1(a)

1(b)

1(c)

1(d)

1(e)

1(f)

# TEKKI SANDAN

1(g)

1(h)

**Application 2**

2(a)

2(b)

2(c)

2(d)

**Application 3**

3(a)

3(b)

3(c)

3(d)

3(e)

3(f)

# TEKKI SANDAN

**Application 4**

4(a)

4(b)

4(c)

4(d)

4(e)

4(f)

*The Advanced Shotokan Karate Handbook*

4(g)

4(h)

4(i)

## Application 5

5(a)

5(b)

5(c)

5(d)

## Application 6

6(a)

6(b)

6(c)

6(d)

6(e)

**Application 7**

7(a)

7(b)

# TEKKI SANDAN

7(c)

7(d)

7(e)

# UNSU

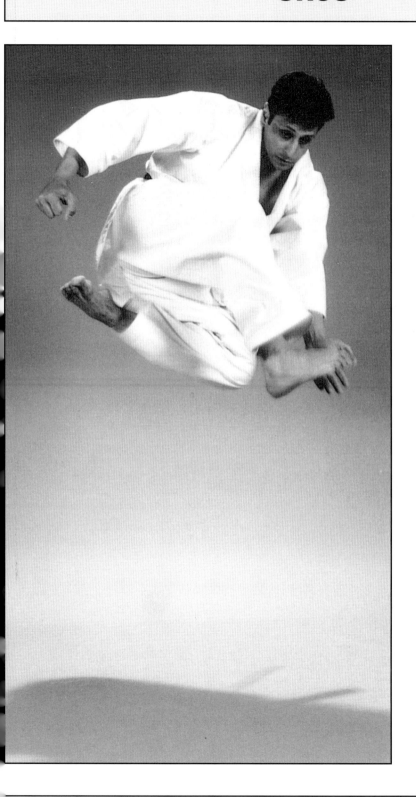

This kata is extremely old and of Chinese origin. The name means 'cloud hands' and the movements resemble clouds in a storm joining together in thunder.

This kata covers several unusual techniques. One whereby you drop to the ground and kick Mawashi Geri, is not normally a wise thing to do when defending yourself against an attacker; but you would certainly have the element of surprise on your side. This kata also consists of a 360 degree jump.

Mainly a kata to be practised by higher Dan grade levels.

# UNSU

(a). Shizentai

(b). Intermediate movement

(c). YOI
Heisoku Dachi

(d). Intermediate movement

1(a). Intermediate movement

2. Neko Ashi Dachi
Morote Keito Uke

2(a). Migi Ippon Nukite

3. Neko Ashi Dachi
Keito Gamae

*The Advanced Shotokan Karate Handbook*

(e). Intermediate
movement

(f). Intermediate
movement

(g). Intermediate
movement

1. Heisoku Dachi
Morote Seiryuto Uke

3(a). Intermediate
movement

3(b). Intermediate
movement

4. Neko Ashi Dachi
Ashi Gake Morote
Keito Uke

4(a). Neko Ashi Dachi
Hidari Ippon Nukite

5. Neko Ashi Dachi
   Keito Gamae

5(a). Intermediate
      movement

5(b). Intermediate
      movement

6. Neko Ashi Dachi
   Ashi Gake Morote Keito
   Uke

8(a). Intermediate
      movement

8(b). Zenkutsu Dachi
      Migi Tate Shuto Uke

9. Zenkutsu Dachi
   Hidari Chudan Gyaku
   Zuki

9(a). Intermediate
      movement

*The Advanced Shotokan Karate Handbook*

6(a). Neko Ashi Dachi
    Migi Ippon Nukite

7. Neko Ashi Dachi
    Keito Gamae

7(a). Zenkutsu Dachi
    Hidari Tate Shuto
    Uke

8. Zenkutsu Dachi
    Migi Chudan Gyaku Zuki

9(b). Zenkutsu Dachi
    Hidari Tate Shuto
    Uke

10. Zenkutsu Dachi
    Migi Chudan Gyaku
    Zuki

10(a). Intermediate
    movement

10(b). Zenkutsu Dachi
    Migi Tate Shuto
    Uke

11. Zenkutsu Dachi Hidari Chudan Gyaku Zuki

11(a). Intermediate movement

11(b). Migi Tai Otoshi

11(c). Hidari Mawashi Geri

13. Intermediate movement

13(a). Intermediate movement

13(b). Intermediate movement

13(c). Intermediate movement

12. Intermediate movement

12(a). Intermediate movement

12(b). Hidari Tai Otoshi

12(c). Migi Mawashi Geri

14. Kiba Dachi
Morote Seiryuto Uke

14(a). Front view

14(b). Intermediate movement

14(c). Intermediate movement

15. Zenkutsu Dachi
    Hidari Keito Uke
    Migi Ushiro Teisho Barai

15(a). Intermediate
       movement
       Side view

15(b). Intermediate
       movement

15(c). Side view

16(b). Intermediate
       movement

17. Zenkutsu Dachi
    Hidari Jodan Haito
    Uchi

17(a). Intermediate
       movement

17(b). Jodan Maegeri

15(d). Intermediate movement

15(e). Side view

16. Zenkutsu Dachi
Migi Keito Uke
Hidari Tcisho Barai

16(a). Side view

17(c). Side view

17(d). Intermediate movement

17(e). Jodan Soto Uke

17(f). Side view

18. Zenkutsu Dachi Hidari Chudan Gyaku Zuki

18(a). Side view

18(b). Intermediate movement

18(c). Side view

19(d). Side view

20. Zenkutsu Dachi Migi Chudan Gyaku Zuki

20(a). Side view

20(b). Pulling left foot back

19. Zenkutsu Dachi
Migi Jodan Haito Uchi

19(a). Jodan Mae Geri

19(b). Intermediate
movement

19(c). Jodan Soto Uke

21. Heisoku Dachi
Ryowan Gamae

21(a). Intermediate
movement

21(b). Intermediate
movement

21(c). Intermediate
movement

22. Zenkutsu Dachi
Migi Gedan Oi Zuki

22(a). Intermediate
movement

23. Zenkutsu Dachi
Hidari Gedan Zuki

23(a). Intermediate
movement

26. Teisho Tate Hasami
Uchi

26(a). Raising knee up

26(b). Gedan Mae
Kekomi Geri
**\*KIAI\***

26(c). Zenkutsu Dachi
Hidari Chudan
Gyaku Zuki

*The Advanced Shotokan Karate Handbook*

24. Zenkutsu Dachi
    Migi Gedan Zuki

24(a). Intermediate
       movement

25. Fudo Dachi
    Chudan Tate Shuto
    Uke

25(a). Intermediate
       movement

27. Zenkutsu Dachi
    Migi Chudan Jung
    Zuki

27(a). Intermediate
       movement

28. Kiba Dachi
    Migi Sokumen Gedan
    Barai

28(a). Back view

# UNSU

28(b). Intermediate
movement

29. Kiba Dachi
Hidari Sokumen
Jodan Haito Uke

29(a). Intermediate
movement

30. Kiba Dachi
Hidari Sokumen Gedan
Shuto Barai

32. Kiba Dachi
Sokumen Gyaku Zuki

32(a). Front view

32(b). Intermediate
movement

32(c). Front view

*The Advanced Shotokan Karate Handbook*

30(a).  Front view

30(b).  Intermediate movement

30(c).  Front view

31.  Migi Sokumen Jodan Haito Uke

33.  Kokutsu Dachi Chudan Haishu Uke

33(a).  Side view

33(b).  Intermediate movement 360° jump

33(c).  Mika Zuki Tobi Geri

33(d). Intermediate movement

33(e). Intermediate movement

34. Ryo Te Fuse

34(a). Front view

34(f). Intermediate movement Sanchin Dachi

34(g). Front view

35. Mawashi Kake Uke

35(a). Front view

34(b). Intermediate movement

34(c). Front view

34(d). Intermediate movement

34(e). Front view

35(b). Intermediate movement

35(c). Intermediate movement

35(d). Intermediate movement
Sanchin Dachi
Mawashi Kake Uke

35(e). Front view

35(f). Front view

36. Sanchin Dachi
Awase Teisho Zuki

36(a). Front view

37(b). Shizentai

37(c). YAME

36(b). Intermediate movement

36(c). Zenkutsu Dachi Hidari Jodan Age Uke

37. Zenkutsu Dachi Migi Chudan Gyaku Zuki **KIAI**

37(a). Shizentai

**Application 1**

1(a)

1(b)

1(c)

1(d)

1(e)

**Application 2**

2(a)

2(b)

2(c)

2(d)

2(e)

**Application 3**

3(a)

3(b)

3(c)

3(d)

3(e)

3(f)

**Application 4**

4(a)

4(b)

4(c)

4(d)

4(e)

4(f)

# UNSU

4(g)

*Preparing for Kumite Final 1978*

# GENERAL INFORMATION

**TISKA Club Photographs**

**Oath of the Dojo**

**Glossary**

**English – Japanese Numbering**

# TISKA CLUB PHOTOGRAPHS

# TISKA CLUB PHOTOGRAPHS

*The Advanced Shotokan Karate Handbook*

# TISKA CLUB PHOTOGRAPHS

# DOJO KUN

## THE DOJO KARATEKA OATH
### "Dojo Kun"

•

### "Hitotsu! Jinkaku Kansei ni Tsutomuru Koto"
*(One! To Strive For The Perfection of Character!)*

•

### "Hitotsu! Makoto No Michi O Mamoru Koto!"
*(One! To Defend The Paths Of Truth!)*

•

### "Hitotsu! Doryoku No Seishin O Yashinau Koto!
*(One! To Foster The Spirit Of Effort!)*

•

### "Hitotsu! Reigi O Omonzuru Koto!"
*(One! To Honour The Principles of Etiquette!)*

•

### "Hitotsu! Kekki No Yu O Imashimuru Koto!"
*(One To Guard Against Impetuous Courage!)*

---

# GLOSSARY

**Age Uke:** *Upper Rising Block*
**Age Zuki:** *Upper Rising Punch*
**Aka:** *Red*
**Ashi Barai:** *Leg Sweep*
**Ashibo Kake Uke:** *Leg Hooking Block*
**Ashikubi Kake Uke:** *Ankle Hooking Block*
**Ashikubi:** *Ankle*
**Ate Waza:** *Smashing Technique*
**Awase:** *Combined*
**Awase Zuki:** *U-Punch*

**Bassai Dal:** *To Storm a Fortress (KATA)*

**Choku Zuki:** *Straight Punch*
**Chudan:** *Middle Level*

**Dachi:** *Middle Level*
**Dan:** *Level*
**Do:** *The Way*
**Dojo:** *Place of the Way, Training Place*

**Empi:** *Elbow*
**Empi Uchi:** *Circle Foot Block*
**Enoy:** *Relax*
**Enpi:** *Flying Swallow (KATA)*

**Fudo Dachi:** *Rooted Stance*
**Fumikomi:** *Stamping Kick*
**Fumikiri:** *Cutting Kick*

**Gaiwan:** *Outer Arm*
**Gankaku:** *Crane on a Rock (KATA)*
**Gedan:** *Lower Level*
**Gedan Barai Uke:** *Lower Level Sweeping Block*
**Gedan Zuki:** *Lower Level Punch*
**Geri:** *Kick*
**Gi:** *Training Suit*
**Gohon Kumite:** *Five Step Sparring*
**Gyaku:** *Reverse*
**Gyaku Kansetsu:** *Against the Joint*
**Gyaku Zuki:** *Reverse Punch*
**Gyaku Mawashi Geri:** *Reverse Round Kick*

**Hachiji Dachi:** *Natural, Open Leg Stance*
**Hai:** *Yes*

**Hajime:** *Start*
**Haiwan:** *Back Arm*
**Haiwan Nagashi Uke:** *Back Arm Sweeping Block*
**Haito:** *Ridge Hand*
**Haito Uchi:** *Ridge Hand Strike*
**Hangetsu:** *Half Moon (KATA)*
**Hangetsu Dachi:** *Half Moon Stance*
**Hanmi:** *Half Front Facing Position*
**Hara:** *Lower Abdomen*
**Hasami Zuki:** *Scissors Punch*
**Heiko Dachi:** *Parallel Stance*
**Heiko Zuki:** *Parallel Punch*
**Heisoku Dachi:** *Informal Attention Stance*
**Hidari:** *Left*
**Hidari Shizen Tai:** *Left Natural Position*
**Hiraken:** *Fore Knucke Fist*
**Hiraken Zuki:** *Fore Knucke Fist Straight Punch*
**Hiza:** *Knee*
**Hiza Geri:** *Knee Kick*
**Hizagashira:** *Knee Cap*
**Hombu:** *Main Dojo Headquarters*
**Hyosh:** *Timing*

**Iee Iie:** *No*
**Ippon:** *One Point*
**Ippon Ken:** *One Knuckle Fist*
**Ippon Ken Zuki:** *One Knuckle Fist Straight Punch*
**Ippon Nukite:** *One Finger Spear Hand*

**Jion:** *From The Temple Of Jion (KATA)*
**Jitte:** *Ten Hands (Jutte) KATA*
**Jodan:** *Upper Level*
**Jiyu Dachi:** *Free Stance*
**Jiyu Ippon Kumite:** *Semi Free One Step Sparring*
**Jiyu Kumite:** *Free Sparring*
**Jo Sokutei:** *Raised Sole*
**Juji Uke:** *X Block*

**Ka:** *Person or Practitioner*
**Kage Uke:** *Hooking Block*
**Kage Zuki:** *Hook Punch*
**Kakato:** *Heel*
**Kake Shuto Uke:** *Hooking Knife Hand Block*
**Kake Uke:** *Hooking Block*
**Kakiwake Uke:** *Reverse Wedge Block*

**Kakuto:** *Bent Wrist*
**Kaiten:** *Rotating*
**Kamaete:** *Action – Take Up Position*
**Kanku Dai:** *Viewing The Sky (KATA)*
**Kara:** *Empty – Chinese*
**Kata:** *Formal Exercise*
**Keage Geri:** *Snap Kick*
**Kebanashi:** *Kick Off*
**Kekomi Geri:** *Thrust*
**Ken:** *Fist*
**Ki:** *Spirit, Inner Power*
**Kiai:** *Shout used to help Ki and Physical Power*
**Kiba Dachi:** *Straddle Leg or Horse Riding Stance*
**Kihon:** *Basic Techniques*
**Kihon Ippon Kumite:** *Basic One Step Sparring*
**Kime:** *Focus*
**Kin Geri:** *Groin Kick*
**Kizami Uke:** *Jabbing Punch*
**Kokutsu Dachi:** *Back Stance*
**Koshi:** *Ball of the Foot*
**Kumite:** *Sparring*
**Kun:** *Motto or Oath*
**Kyu:** *Grade*

**Ma-Ai:** *Distancing*
**Mae:** *Front*
**Mae Geri:** *Front Kick*
**Maeude Deai Osae:** *Forearm Pressing Block*
**Maeude Hineri Uke:** *Forearm Twist Block*
**Makiwara:** *Striking Post*
**Mawashi Geri:** *Roundhouse Kick*
**Mawashi Zuki:** *Roundhouse Punch*
**Mawate:** *Turn*
**Migi:** *Right Side*
**Migzuki Geri:** *Crescent Kick*
**Mokuso:** *Meditation*
**Morote Uke:** *Augmented Block*
**Morote Zuki:** *Augmented Punch*
**Morote Tzukami Uki:** *Two Handed Grasping Block*
**Moto Dachi:** *Original Stance*
**Musubi Dachi:** *Informal Attention*

**Nagashi Uke:** *Sweeping Block*
**Naiwan:** *Inner Arm*
**Nakadaka Ippon Ken:** *Middle Finger One Knuckle Fist*
**Nakadaka Ken:** *Middle Finger Knuckle Fist*

# GLOSSARY

**Nami Ashi (Gaeshi):** *Inside Snapping Leg Block*
**Neko Ashi Dachi:** *Cat Foot Stance*
**Nidan Geri:** *Double Kick*
**Nihon Nukite:** *Two Finger Spear Hand*
**Nukite:** *Spear Hand*

**Obi:** *Belt, Sash*
**Oi Zuki:** *Stepping Punch*
**Okinawa Te:** *Okinawan School of Karate*
**Osae:** *Pressing*
**Otoshi:** *Dropping*

**Rei:** *Bow*
**Reinoji Dachi:** *L. Stance*
**Ren Zuki:** *Combination Punching*
**Ryo:** *Both*
**Ryu:** *School of Martial Art*

**Sanbon Kumite:** *Three Step Sparring*
**Sanchin Dachi:** *Hour Glass Stance*
**Sash Ashi:** *Stepping Across/ Extending the Foot*
**Seiken:** *Fore Fist*
**Seiza:** *Kneeling Position (Meditation Posture)*
**Seiyuto:** *Ox Jaw Hand*
**Seiryuto Uke:** *Ox Jaw Block*
**Sempai:** *Senior*
**Sensei:** *Teacher*
**Shihan:** *Master*
**Shusin:** *Referee*
**Shiro:** *White*
**Sinzentai:** *Natural Stance*
**Shirho Wari:** *Breaking Boards on four side to test power*

**Shiko Dachi:** *Square Stance*
**Shobu:** *Competition*
**Shuto:** *Knife Hand*
**Shuto Uchi:** *Knife Hand Strike*
**Sochin Dachi:** *Diagonal Straddle Leg Stance*
**Sokumen:** *Side*
**Sokutei Mawashi Uke:** *Circular Sole Block*
**Sokuto:** *Edge of the Foot*
**Sokuto Osai Uke:** *Pressing block with foot edge*
**Sukui Uke:** *Scooping Block*
**Soto Ude Uke:** *Outside Forearm Block*

**Tai Sabaki:** *Body Shifting*
**Tameshiwari:** *Testing by Breaking*
**Tanden:** *Navel*
**Tate Empi Uchi:** *Upward Elbow Strike*
**Tate Shuto Uke:** *Vertical Knife Hand Block*
**Tate Zuki:** *Vertical Fist Punch*
**Te:** *Hand*
**Teisho:** *Palm Heel*
**Teisho Awase Uke:** *Combined Palm Heel Block*
**Teisho Uchi:** *Palm Heel Strike*
**Teisho Uke:** *Palm Heel Block*
**Teiji Dach:** *T Stance*
**Tekubi:** *Wrist*
**Tettsui:** *Bottom Fist*
**Te Nagashi Uke:** *Hand Sweeping Block*
**Te Osae Uke:** *Hand Pressing Block*
**Te Waza:** *Hand Technique*
**Tobi:** *Jumping*
**Tobi Tettsui Uchi:** *Jumping*

*Hammer Fist Strike*
**Tokui:** *Favourite*
**Tsukami:** *Grasping*
**Tsumasaki:** *Tips of (Toes/Fingers)*
**Tsuru Ashi Dachi:** *Crane Leg Stance*

**Uchi:** *Strike*
**Uchi Ude Uke:** *Inside Forearm Block*
**Uchi Hachiji Dachi:** *Inverted Open Leg Stance*
**Uchi Waza:** *Striking Techniques*
**Ude:** *Forearm*
**Uke:** *Block*
**Ura Zuki:** *Close Punch*
**Uraken:** *Back Fist*
**Ushiro Geri:** *Back Kick*
**Ushiro Empi Uchi:** *Back Elbow Uchi*

**Wa:** *Harmony*
**Wan:** *Arm*
**Wanto:** *Sword*
**Washide:** *Eagle Hand*
**Waza:** *Techniques, Skills*

**Yama Zuki:** *Wide U Punch*
**Yame:** *Stop*
**Yoi:** *Ready*
**Yoko:** *Side*
**Yoko Empi:** *Side Elbow*
**Yoko Empi Uchi:** *Side Elbow Strike*
**Yoko Geri:** *Side Kick*

**Zanshin:** *Mental Alertness*
**Za Zen:** *Zen Meditation (Usually Seated)*

# THE ENGLISH – JAPANESE NUMBERING TABLES 1–100

| | | |
|---|---|---|
| 1 – ICHI | 35 – SANJYU GO | 69 – ROKUJYU KU |
| 2 – NI | 36 – SANJYU ROKU | 70 – SHICHIJYU |
| 3 – SAN | 37 – SANJYU SHICHI | 71 – SHICHIJYU ICHI |
| 4 – SHI | 38 – SANJYU HACHI | 72 – SHICHIJYU NI |
| 5 – GO | 39 – SANJYU KU | 73 – SHICHIJYU SAN |
| 6 – ROKU | 40 – YONJYU | 74 – SHICHIJYU SHI |
| 7 – SHICHI | 41 – YONJYU ICHI | 75 – SHICHIJYU GO |
| 8 – HACHI | 42 – YONJYU NI | 76 – SHICHIJYU ROKU |
| 9 – KU | 43 – YONJYU SAN | 77 – SHICHIJYU SHICHI |
| 10 – JYU | 44 – YONJYU SHI | 78 – SHICHIJYU HACHI |
| 11 – JYU ICHI | 45 – YONJYU GO | 79 – SHICHIJYU KU |
| 12 – JYU NI | 46 – YONJYU ROKU | 80 – HACHIJYU |
| 13 – JYU SAN | 47 – YONJYU SHICHI | 81 – HACHIJYU ICHI |
| 14 - JYU SHI | 48 – YONJYU HACHI | 82 – HACHIJYU NI |
| 15 – JYU GO | 49 – YONJYU KU | 83 – HACHIJYU SAN |
| 16 – JYU ROKU | 50 – GOJYU | 84 – HACHIJYU SHI |
| 17 – JYU SHICHI | 51 – GOJYU ICHI | 85 – HACHIJYU GO |
| 18 – JYU HACHI | 52 – GOJYU NI | 86 – HACHIJYU ROKU |
| 19 – JYU KU | 53 – GOJYU SAN | 87 – HACHIJYU SHICHI |
| 20 – NIJYU | 54 – GOJYU SHI | 88 – HACHIJYU HACHI |
| 21 – NIJYU ICHI | 55 – GOJYU GO | 89 – HACHIJYU KU |
| 22 – NIJYU NI | 56 – GOJYU ROKU | 90 – KYUJYU |
| 23 – NIJYU SAN | 57 – GOJYU SHICHI | 91 – KYUJYU ICHI |
| 24 – NIJYU SHI | 58 – GOJYU HACHI | 92 – KYUJYU NI |
| 25 – NIJYU GO | 59 – GOJYU KU | 93 – KYUJYU SAN |
| 26 – NIJYU ROKU | 60 – ROKUJYU | 94 – KYUJYU SHI |
| 27 – NIJYU SHICHI | 61 – ROKUJYU ICHI | 95 – KYUJYU GO |
| 28 – NIJYU HACHI | 62 – ROKUJYU NI | 96 – KYUJYU ROKU |
| 29 – NIJYU KU | 63 – ROKUJYU SAN | 97 – KYUJYU SHICHI |
| 30 – SANJYU | 64 – ROKUJYU SHI | 98 – KYUJYU HACHI |
| 31 – SANJYU ICHI | 65 – ROKUJYU GO | 99 – KYUJYU KU |
| 32 – SANJYU NI | 66 – ROKUJYU ROKU | 100 – HYAKU |
| 33 – SANJYU SAN | 67 – ROKUJYU SHICHI | |
| 34 – SANJYU SHI | 68 – ROKUJYU HACHI | |

# YOUR

## Chance to
## own your
## personal grading
## syllabus from

## Beginner to Black Belt

## www.tiska.com

# YOU'VE READ THE BOOKS –
# NOW SEE THE FILMS

This unique set of videos has been produced by Sensei Gursharan Sahota, Chief Instructor of the Traditional International Shotokan Karate Association – which compliment his books – *The Shotokan Karate Handbook - Beginner to Black Belt* and *The Advanced Shotokan Karate Handbook.*

Having initially produced the videos for students of his own Association Sensei Sahota rapidly realised the benefits that other karate-ka could gain from developing basic standards and grading technique with the aid of these films. The intention of the videos, however, is to encourage and help karate-ka to undertake the required practice at home and **not** to replace regular training of a student's own Sensei.

---

*Above:* Karate v Cancer. In 1996 over 750 students of TISKA led by Sensei Sahota raised over £10,000 through a one day charity event for St John's Home, Moggerhanger – a Sue Ryder Home.

*Right:* Sensei Sahota with some of the Junior Members of TISKA in South Africa.

*Below:* Young Sensei – The National Championships of 1976